Ralph J. Bunche

Peacemaker

Patricia and Fredrick McKissack

Illustrated by Ned O.

❖ *Great African Americans Series* ❖

ENSLOW PUBLISHERS, INC.

Bloy St. & Ramsey Ave.   Box 38
Box 777   Aldershot
Hillside, N.J. 07205   Hants GU12 6BP
U.S.A.   U.K.

For Nancy and Paul Polette

Library of Congress Cataloging-in-Publication Data

McKissack, Pat, 1944-
    Ralph J. Bunche: peacemaker / Patricia and Fredrick McKissack.
        p. cm. — (Great African-Americans series)
    Includes Index.
    Summary: Biography of the African-American statesman and diplomat who was one of the founders of the United Nations and who received the Nobel Prize for his peacemaking efforts.
    ISBN 0-89490-300-4
    1. Bunche, Ralph J. (Ralph Johnson), 1904-1971—Juvenile literature. 2. Statesman—United States—Biography—Juvenile literature. 3. United Nations—History—Juvenile literature.
[1. Bunche, Ralph J. (Ralph Johnson), 1904-1971. 2. Statesman. 3. Afro-Americans—Biography.] I. McKissack, Fredrick. II. Title. III. Series.
E748.B885M38 1991
341.23'3'092—dc20
[B]   90-49849
[92]   CIP
                                         AC
Printed in the United States of America
10 9 8 7 6 5 4 3 2 1

Photo Credits: National Archives, p. 27; Schomburg Center for Research in Black Culture/The New York Public Library/Astor, Lenox and Tilden Foundations, p. 25; The United Nations, p. 4; Department of Special Collections, the University Library, The University of California, Los Angeles, pp. 8, 10, 13, 19, 22.

Illustration Credits: Ned O., pp. 6, 7, 12, 14, 17, 23, 28.

Cover Illustration: Ned O.

Contents

Dr. Ralph Bunche
Born: August 7, 1904, Detroit, Michigan.
Died: December 9, 1971, New York, New York.

1

What a World!

Ralph Johnson Bunche was born in 1904. He grew up in a large, loving family. He lived with his parents, aunts, uncle, and grandmother in a small house.

Grandmother Nana was Ralph's favorite family member.

The family was poor, but they were proud people—and happy, too. Ralph grew up believing in himself. He also loved to learn.

When Ralph was eleven years old his

family moved to New Mexico. His favorite teacher was Miss Emma Belle Sweet.

She taught about different countries and the people who lived there. What a wonderful world! Ralph wanted to visit all the places on the map.

When Ralph's mother and father died,

Nana moved the family to Los Angeles, California. Ralph entered school. He also found a job selling papers.

One day Ralph and the other boys were taken on a picnic and swim party. A sign on the pool gate said "No **colored*** allowed." Ralph could not swim. What a terrible world!

---

* Words in **bold type** are explained in *Words to Know* on page 30.

Ralph told Nana what happened. She would not let him feel sorry for himself, "You are as good as anybody. Remember that!" she said. It was not always easy to remember.

Ralph's grades were the highest in his class. He was sure he would be asked to

Jefferson High School class of 1922. Ralph is the last boy on the right. Some people were surprised a black student could do so well in school. Nana wasn't surprised.

join the **honor society**. Ralph listened for his name. It wasn't called. He wanted to quit school. Nana wouldn't hear of it! "You are as good as anybody." Ralph **graduated** from Jefferson High School with highest honors. He gave the class speech.

Nana had been right. Being poor had not stopped Ralph. Losing his parents had not stopped him. The color of his skin had not stopped him. What a wonderful world!

Ralph liked all sports. He played basketball, baseball, and football at UCLA. Still his grades were the highest in the class of 1927.

2

A Real Winner

Ralph's good grades helped him get into the University of California at Los Angeles (UCLA). He worked hard and studied long hours. And he was a winner in most things he tried.

Ralph played on the UCLA basketball team. It was a winning team. Ralph liked to help his team win. He was a member of other school clubs and groups. Again, his grades were very good, so he finished

UCLA with high honors—another victory!

Then on to Harvard University...maybe!

His good grades won Ralph the money to attend Harvard in Massachusetts. But,

it was not enough to pay for books, food, or rent. He could not go to school.

But a woman's club in Los Angeles raised $1000 for Ralph to go to school. In the fall of 1927, Ralph entered Harvard.

There he worked hard and studied long hours. Nana wrote often. Then Aunt Nelle

Ralph (third from left) was well-liked at Harvard. He did many different jobs to earn money for school. Sometimes his shoes had holes. His shirts were old. But he was always clean.

called to say Nana had died. It was a very sad time. He would remember his loving Nana's words, "You are as good as anybody."

In 1928 Ralph Bunche finished his studies in government. Then, he taught at Howard University in Washington, D.C.

That's where he met Ruth Harris, a pretty school teacher. Soon he won her heart, and they were married in the spring of 1930.

Ralph Bunche was happy. He felt like a real winner!

3

Nations for Peace

Between 1932 and 1934 Ralph studied in Africa. Ralph's long studies and hard work in Africa earned him a Ph.D., or advanced degree. Now he could be called Dr. Ralph Bunche!

Dr. Bunche studied a subject called **political science**. Political science is the study of governments. Dr. Bunche was the first African American to earn this kind of degree from Harvard University. Nana would have been so proud.

Dr. Bunche wanted to learn more about Africa. An African friend told him to visit his people, the Kikuyu (key-KOO-yu). The Kikuyu live in Kenya, an East African country. Dr. Bunche went there.

The Kikuyu treated Dr. Bunche like a son who had been lost. He told them that

his family had come from Africa a long time ago. The Kikuyu gave Dr. Bunche a Kikuyu name: Karioki, (Ka-ree-o-kee) which means, "He who has returned from the dead." It was like a big party to say "You have come home."

Then World War II began. The countries of the world were at war. Ralph was asked to work for the State Department. At last the war ended.

Millions of people died in the war. Millions more were sure to die if the world did not work to keep peace. Between 1944 and 1946, the **United Nations** (the **UN**) was begun. Nations came together for peace. Dr. Bunche had a part in the founding of the United Nations.

It was decided that the home of the UN would be in New York. Dr. Bunche was

Dr. Bunche often spoke with African leaders. He studied all over Africa. Once, he even went to Capetown University in South Africa.

asked to work at the UN. The Bunches moved to New York.

During World War II, millions of Jews had been put to death. The Jewish people had no country of their own. The United Nations set aside a piece of land for the Jews. This was to become the country of Israel.

There were many people living in and around Israel who didn't want Israel to become a country. Five **Arab** countries attacked Israel in the spring of 1948. There was war in the **Holy Land**!

4

Peace Gets a Chance

The Arab-Israeli War was the first real test of the UN. Could the UN really help stop wars? The leaders at the UN put together the best team they could. Count Folke Bernadotte (BUR-nuh-daht) from Sweden led the team. Dr. Bunche was chosen to help Count Bernadotte.

The count asked the Israelis and the Arabs to meet on a Greek island. They would not come. But the count didn't give up. Peace must get a chance.

It took four weeks, but the armies stopped fighting at last. It was a beginning. Would peace last?

Then, in September 1948, Count Bernadotte was killed. Would his death

The UN sent troops to the Middle East to keep peace. Dr. Bunche visited the troops in 1949. He told them he hoped the fighting would end forever.

stop the peace talks? It was a dark day for peace. The world was sad.

Dr. Bunche was asked to keep working for peace. War between Israel and the Arabs started again. But, Dr. Bunche didn't give up. Peace must get a chance.

There were months and months of

talking. Finally the Israelis and the Arabs ended the war. A **peace treaty** was signed.

Peace at last!

Dr. Bunche gave each Israeli and Arab at the meeting a peace gift—a beautiful piece of **pottery**. "What if we had not made peace?" one of the Israelis asked.

"I would have hit you over the head with them," Dr. Bunche answered, smiling. Then everyone laughed.

Peace would get a chance at last.

5

He Was the First

Being at home with his wife Ruth and his family meant more to Dr. Bunche than being well-known. But he was a hero. People loved him. They wanted to meet him and to hear him speak. Pictures of Dr. Bunche and his family were in newspapers and on the covers of magazines.

Los Angeles had a Ralph Bunche Day and a big parade. His name was added to the city honor society. It would have meant so much more if his name had been

Dr. Bunche liked being home with his family. He had three children: Joan and Ralph, Jr., pictured here, and Jane.

added in 1922. But, he smiled and said, "Thank you."

Winning a **Nobel Peace Prize** is one of the highest honors given in the world. In 1950, Ralph Bunche won the Nobel Peace Prize for helping end the war in the Holy

Dr. Bunche received the Nobel Peace Prize. He also won many other honors. In 1949, the National Association for the Advancement of Colored People (NAACP) gave him their highest **award**.

Land. He was the first African American to win this high honor.

He also was given the **Gold Key Award** by the **National Education Association**. Dr. Bunche was asked to name his favorite teacher. Who else but Miss Emma Belle Sweet!

Was Miss Sweet still alive? Yes. She was 82 years old. But, she was able to

come to receive the Gold Key given to her. Dr. Bunche got to see his favorite teacher again after 47 years.

Dr. Ralph Johnson Bunche worked for the UN and peace for 25 years. He was a man of firsts...the first member of his family to finish college...the first black man to earn an advanced degree in political science from Harvard University... and the first black man to win the Nobel Peace Prize. He did it against all odds.

In 1971 Dr. Bunche left the UN because his health was poor. He died six months later on December 9, 1971. The world was sad. A news reporter wrote: "...when all the world praises a man there seems little left to say."

Words to Know

award—An honor given to a person for doing something special.

Arab—A group of people living in the Middle East and North Africa.

colored—An outdated name that was used for African-Americans.

degree—A school gives a degree (a title) to a person who has completed all their studies.

Gold Key Award—An honor given to a person who has done an outstanding job in the area of education.

graduate (GRAJ-uh-wait)—To complete studies at a school and earn a degree. *See* degree.

Holy Land—Countries in the Middle East where the Jewish, Christian, and Islamic religions began.

honor society (AH-ner so-SY-uh-tee)—a group of people who have earned very high grades in school.

National Education Association—An organization of people who work in education, like teachers, principals, and others.

Nobel Peace Prize—A special honor given to a person who has worked for world peace. It is named after Alfred Nobel, the man who left money in his will to start the prize.

peace treaty—An agreement that stops war or keeps war from starting.

political science (puh-LIT-i-kull SY-ents)—The study of governments and how they work.

pottery— Things made of clay like some pots, bowls, plates, and cups.

United Nations—An organization of many countries who work together for peace.

Index